www.FlowerpotPress.com
DJS-0912-0101
ISBN: 978-1-68461-098-3
Made in China/Fabriqué en Chine

THE STORY OF CHRISTMAS

Illustrated by Pascale Lafond

A long time ago, a very special man lived in a town called Nazareth. He taught us to live in love and harmony, to be kind to each other, to love and worship God, and to look forward to life everlasting. His name was Jesus. We celebrate His birth every year at Christmas.

The is the Christmas story—the story of the birth of Jesus Christ.

The Baby Jesus was born of a woman named Mary. Mary was engaged to a carpenter named Joseph. Mary was a good woman and Joseph was a good man. They both loved each other very much and looked forward to being married.

One day, God sent an angel to visit Mary and bring her very important news. The angel's name was Gabriel. Gabriel said:

"Do not be afraid. I am here to tell you that you have found favor with God. You are blessed. You will conceive a child, a son, and when He is born, you will call Him Jesus. He will be the Son of God, and He will bring salvation to all the world."

When Mary heard this, her heart filled with joy.

When Joseph heard Mary was going to have a baby, he was upset. He loved Mary but thought that he should not marry her. Then an angel appeared to him in a dream and said:

"Joseph, do not be afraid. You can still take Mary as your wife, for the child she has conceived has come to her through the Holy Spirit. Mary is a good woman. She will have a baby son and you shall call Him Jesus. Jesus will save the world."

When Joseph awoke, he felt better. He did what the angel told him, and he and Mary were married.

The town of Nazareth, where Mary and Joseph lived, was ruled at that time by an emperor in Rome. The emperor decreed that a census be taken of every person in the Roman Empire.

Joseph was required to go to Bethlehem, for he was from the line of David and this was where they were to be counted. So even though Mary was pregnant with Baby Jesus, Joseph and Mary had to travel all the way to the little town of Bethlehem.

When they arrived in Bethlehem, Joseph and Mary knew she was going to have the Baby Jesus soon, so they tried to stay at the inn. However, because so many people had come to the town for the census, there was no room at the inn. When they realized they could not find a proper room, they ended up staying in a small stable.

It was in that small stable that the Baby Jesus was born. Mary and Joseph made a bed for Jesus by wrapping Him in cloth and laying Him in a manger.

Out in the fields there were shepherds watching their flocks. An angel appeared to them and the glory of the Lord shone around them. They were afraid, but the angel said to them:

"Be not afraid, for, behold, I bring you tidings of great joy for all people. For unto you is born this day in the city of David a Savior, who is Christ the Lord. And this shall be a sign unto you; Ye shall find the babe wrapped in swaddling clothes lying in a manger."

Then suddenly, there with the angel was a multitude of the heavenly host praising God and saying:

"Glory to God in the highest,
and peace to His people on Earth."

When the shepherds heard this news, they headed for Bethlehem right away.

Also at the time Jesus was born, there were three wise men, known as Magi, who were in the East. They saw a star in the night that they knew to be His star. They knew this star signaled the birth of Christ the King. Knowing the significance of this star, the Magi set on their way to find Jesus.

Mary and Joseph were enjoying time alone with Jesus, but soon they would have many visitors wishing to celebrate the birth of Baby Jesus.

Baby Jesus had many visitors! They came to see the Son of God and savior of all mankind. The shepherds came first, and then the three wise men came with their gifts of gold, frankincense, and myrrh. When they saw Jesus, they were overjoyed. This was the first Christmas celebration.

Throughout His life, Jesus spread the good news of God's love. He spoke of God's love to many people, performed miracles, and brought joy to countless followers and believers. He taught us to love God and to love one another. His message is the most important message we ever learn. And His story is the true story of Christmas.

It is the story of how He came to bring
PEACE ON EARTH.